Riddle Riot

Lori Miller Fox

Illustrated by Sanford Hoffman

Sterling Publishing Co., Inc.
New York

Library of Congress Cataloging-in-Publication Data Available

10 9 8 7 6 5 4 3 2 1

Published in 2003 by Sterling Publishing Co., Inc.
387 Park Avenue South, New York, NY 10016
©1991 by Lori Miller Fox
Orginally published under the title *Riddlemania*
Distributed in Canada by Sterling Publishing
$^{c}/o$ Canadian Manda Group, One Atlantic Avenue, Suite 105
Toronto, Ontario, Canada M6K 3E7
Distributed in Great Britain and Europe by Chris Lloyd at Orca Book
Services, Stanley House, Fleets Lane, Poole BH15 3AJ, England
Distributed in Australia by Capricorn Link (Australia) Pty. Ltd.
P.O. Box 704, Windsor, NSW 2756, Australia

Sterling ISBN 1-4027-0825-4

Contents

Believe It or Nuts

How do angels greet each other?
They wave halo.

What does a one-legged turkey say?
"Hobble-hobble."

Where do scoundrels enlist?
In the Knave-y.

How do baby fish know how to swim?
Finstinct.

What car runs underwater?
A Scubaru.

What sea serpent solves mysteries?
Sher-lochness Holmes.

Who was the meanest octopus in the Old West?
Billy the Squid.

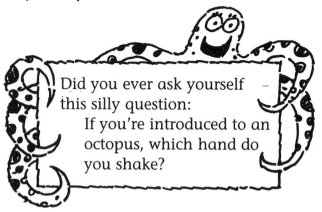

Did you ever ask yourself this silly question:
If you're introduced to an octopus, which hand do you shake?

Who is the fastest detective?
Quick Tracy.

Who is the most forgetful detective?
Dick Spacey.

Who's the meanest ape?
Gorilla the Hun.

Who's the meanest chicken?
Atilla the Hen.

POOH'S WHO?

Who is the silliest bear?
Ninny-the-Pooh.

What bear is white, cuddly, and has curls?
Winnie-the-Poodle.

Who is the smallest bear?
Mini-the-Pooh.

Who is the thinnest bear?
Skinny-the-Pooh.

What would you get if you crossed a bear with a puppy?
Winnie-the-Pooch.

What chickens rob people?
Peck-pockets.

What would you get if you crossed a hen with a four-leaf clover?
A good-cluck charm.

What do you call a Mexican gentleman over 65?
A señor citizen.

What title did the attractive boa constrictor win?
"Hiss Universe."

What's a tyrant's favorite drink?
Cruel-Aid.

What's Scrooge's favorite drink?
Gruel-Aid.

What camera develops underwater pictures immediately?
A Poolaroid.

Where do mice park their boats?
At the hickory dickory dock.

What would you get if you crossed a submarine with a jeep?
A vehicle with 4-whale dive.

Why don't bananas like to sunbathe?
They have a tendency to peel.

What's the tallest plant in France?
The Eiffel Flower.

What did the catcher put outside his front door?
A welcome mitt.

What Jedi loves winter sports?
  Luke Ski-walker.

What do depressed cheerleaders suffer from?
  The sis-boom-blahs.

What pain do many composers suffer from?
  Bach aches.

What songs bore people so much that they fall asleep without even trying?
  Dullabies.

What do babies love to listen to?
  Rock-a-bye 'n' roll music.

What would you get if you crossed a baby with a yogi?

A goo-gooru.

What does the victim of a practical joke send the person who pulled it?

A prank-you note.

Where does Ziggy keep his allowance?

In a Ziggybank.

What crazies hung around the bars of the Old West?

Saloon-atics.

Why did the blue jay get a perm?

Because the curly bird catches the worm.

HIS AND WHOSE?

What do a chocolate lover's towels say?
"His" and "Hershey's."

What do towels on Mount Olympus say?
"His" and "Hercules."

Why did the little bird buy the big bird a greeting card?
For Feather's Day.

Who do birds marry?
Their tweethearts.

Why did the mother parrot scold the baby parrot?
For not talking back.

Why did the groom go to jail?
For not paying his tuxes.

What's the difference between an airplane and a chicken?
An airplane doesn't have any meat on its wing.

Where do you compose complaints?
On a gripewriter.

What do grouchy people fly in?
Com-planes.

What do sneakers do when they're angry?
Stick their tongues out.

What is the largest meteorite?
Whaley's Comet.

2. Zoo's Company

What bear never wants to grow up?
Peter Pan-da.

What is the most boring farm animal?
Blah, blah, black sheep.

What is the meanest farm animal?
The bullygoat.

What is the busiest farm animal?
The mouse. It's always in a scurry.

Why do spiders make good doctors?
They make house crawls.

What do you call a crazy frog?
A croakpot.

Where do goofy frogs sit?
On silly pads.

What is a cat's favorite cartoon series?
"The Fur Side."

How do geese communicate with headquarters?
Over squawkie-talkies.

YOU NAME IT

Where do you find the names of a wide variety of famous animals?
In "Zoo's Who."

Where do you find the names of famous antelopes?
In "Gnu's Who."

Where do you find the names of famous sheep?
In "Ewe's Who."

Where do you find the names of famous owls?
In "Whoooo's Who."

Where do you find the names of famous tropical birds?
In "Cockatoo's Who."

What bird loves to dance ballet?
A cocka-tutu.

What bird can tell time?
A clocka-too.

SHORT AND TWEET

What flies, chirps, and bores itself silly?
A humdrumming bird.

What flies, chirps, and shortens pants?
A hemmingbird.

What flies, chirps, and sings religious songs?
A hymningbird.

Do cats get angry?
Yes, they get fur-ious.

What would you get if you crossed Chicken Little with Kermit?
A frog that peeps as it leaps.

What would you get if you crossed a giraffe with a polar bear?
An animal that wouldn't mind cold weather if it could get a long enough scarf.

What would you get if you crossed a skunk with Ma Bell?

A telephone that you hold up to your ear but away from your nose.

Why aren't moles welcome in banks?

Because they burrow too much.

What would you get if you crossed an alligator with a rooster?

"Croc-a-doodle-do!"

What would you get if you crossed an alligator with a lion?

An animal you don't cross.

What would you get if you crossed an alligator with a pygmy?

A crocodile with a short temper.

How is a rubber band like a crocodile?

If you pull it too hard, it snaps.

How do you get a crocodile on a roller coaster?

Buy him a ticket.

How do you get a crocodile into a fine restaurant?

In a shirt and tie.

Where do cowboys go to ride horses and be impolite?

To a rude-eo.

Where do you gas up a horse?
At a filly station.

What prehistoric creature is huge, yellow, and shaped like a lemon?
A dino-sour.

What do you call a brontosaurus who gets angry when he doesn't win?
A saur loser.

What did the snake give his girlfriend when he escorted her home?
A hiss goodnight.

What reptile can't be trusted?
A rattlesneak.

What would you get if you crossed a rattlesnake with a dog?
A puppy whose bite is MUCH worse than its bark.

What's a dog's favorite sport?
Biscuit-ball.

What kind of dog does Count Dracula have?
A bloodhound.

What kind of dog does Noah have?
A floodhound.

What dogs pick out furniture?
In-terrier decorators.

What do you say when you tickle a puppy?
"Poochie, poochie, coo."

Who did the Irish setter hire to watch her pups?
A baby setter.

What dog is always carrying shopping bags?
A German shlepherd.

What would you get if you crossed a German shepherd with a kid wearing braces?
A dog whose bark is worse than his overbite.

What did the dog say when he stubbed his toe?
"Ow-wow!"

What do you get when you cross a Doberman with a St. Bernard?
A dog that rips your arm off and then runs for help.

What does a yuppie zebra wear?
Pinstripes.

What famous cow wore a feather headdress and smoked a peace pipe?
Geronimoo.

What does Porky do to keep himself busy?
Pigsaw puzzles.

What would you get if you crossed a cheetah with a centipede?

A wildcat that loves to run, but takes too long to put on its sneakers.

SANTA'S LITTLE DEERS

Where do you find the names of Santa's reindeer?
In "Hooves' Who."

Which one of Santa's reindeer sells hats?
Haber-Dasher.

Which one of Santa's reindeer does concerts?
Ma-Donner.

What would you get if you crossed a salmon with a tadpole?

A frog that swims upstream before it croaks.

How do skunks know when to release their terrible smell?

Instink.

What is the most squeamish animal?

An ele-faint.

What would you get if you crossed a PC with an elephant?

A computer with lots of memory.

What would you get if you crossed a dog with an elephant?

I don't know, but you'd better watch out when it jumps on your bed.

What would you get if you crossed an eagle with an elephant?

A two-ton bird that likes to fly but has trouble landing.

When do little gnus chew the furniture?
When they're gnaw-ty.

What large, horned animal never gives up?
A try-noceros.

What large, horned animal never has any fun?
A rhino-serious.

What happens to a rhinoceros' armor when it stays out in the rain too long?
It rhinocerusts.

What would you get if you crossed an insect with a large, horned animal?

A fly-noceros.

What would you get if you crossed a rhinoceros with a snowflake?

I don't know, but you'd better watch out for blizzards.

What would you get if you crossed a bear with a Smurf?

Winnie-the-Blue.

What small ghost talks to Push-Me-Pull-You animals?

Dr. Boolittle.

What rooster talks to Push-Me-Pull-You animals?

Dr. Cock-a-Doolittle-Do.

What did the Push-Me-Pull-You animal say when Dr. Doolittle was being a pest?

"Llama alone."

Eat Your Heart Out

What does a hippie feed his dogs?
Groovy Train.

What does Pinocchio feed his wooden dog?
Puppet Chow.

What does a witch serve her friends?
A full-curse meal.

What chubby little dog makes biscuits?
The Pillsbury Doberman.

What's Santa's favorite sandwich?
Peanut butter and jolly.

What is a cannibal's favorite gourmet dish?
Peasant under glass.

What candy do award-winning television stars eat?
M & Emmies.

What sound does a chicken's cereal make?
"Snap, crackle, peep."

What sound does a barber's cereal make?
"Snip, crackle, pop."

What did the hungry cook say to the pot of pasta?
"Spaghetti or not, here I come."

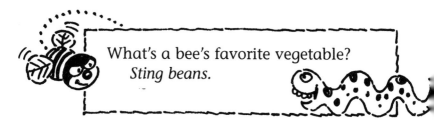

What's a bee's favorite vegetable?
Sting beans.

What's a vegetarian's favorite baseball team?
The Green Giants.

What's the difference between a turkey and a house guest?
One is stuffed before dinner and one is stuffed after dinner.

What's the difference between a peanut and a turtle?
Both have shells, but a peanut is easier to eat.

How do vegetables win a race?
They cross the spinach line.

What's an Inuit's favorite vegetable?
Mushed potatoes.

What's a demolition-derby driver's favorite vegetable?
Smashed potatoes.

BREADTIME STORIES

What do mythical dwarfs make sandwiches on?
Troll wheat bread.

What did President Eisenhower make sandwiches on?
Dwight bread.

What did the camel want its sandwich on?
Humpernickel bread.

What does Muhammad Ali make sandwiches on?
Pumperknuckle bread.

What do babies make sandwiches on?
Pampersnickel bread.

What does Little Miss Longstocking make sandwiches on?
Pippiseed bagels.

BREADTIME STORIES

What do rabbits make sandwiches on?
Hoppyseed bagels.

What does Big Bird make sandwiches on?
Sesame seed buns.

What do comedians make sandwiches on?
Cornybread.

What do wimps make sandwiches on?
Cry bread.

What does a Japanese warrior make sandwiches on?
Samu-rye bread.

What do jockeys make sandwiches on?
Thoroughbread.

What do pizza makers put on their eggs?
Salt and pepper-oni.

Where do you bring a salad that's not yours?
To the Tossed and Found.

What's the messiest vegetable?
Corn on the slob.

What does a slob's Jack-in-the-Box play?
"Slop Goes the Weasel."

What's the scariest vegetable?
Corn on the Blob.

What happens when an onion tells a joke?
You laugh and cry at the same time.

What's a frog's favorite snack?
Croaker Jacks.

What is Kareem Abdul Jabbar's
favorite dessert?
Ice Kareem.

What do you get when someone spills ice cream on
James Bond?
Spy à la mode.

What is a cannibal's favorite dessert?
Tot fudge sundaes.

What's a millionaire's favorite dessert?
Yacht fudge sundaes.

What's an acrobat's favorite pastry?
Apple turnovers.

Where do criminals find the recipe for a cake that
has a file in it?
In a crookbook.

4. The Show Must Go!

Where can you watch *Gone With the Wind* 24 hours a day?

On Gable TV.

What did Aesop watch for entertainment?

Fable TV.

What does a mechanic watch for entertainment?

Jumper cable TV.

What unbelievable stories do bees tell?
Old hives' tales.

Who's the toughest clown?
Rambo-zo.

Who can knit while firing a machine gun?
Grambo.

WHICH IS HITCH?

What movie producer could fly?
Alfred Hitchcock-atoo.

What movie producer was always scratching himself?
Alfred Itchcock.

What movie producer thumbed rides?
Alfred Hitchhike.

Who was the most conceited movie producer?
Alfred Hitchcock-y.

What does a comedian say when he sticks his tongue out in a doctor's office?
"H-ahhhh."

Who gave the Ghost of Christmas Past a cold?
Ebe-sneezer Scrooge.

Who does Curious George become when he's angry?
Furious George.

What does Tarzan play on in the playground?
The jungle gym.

What do you transport films in?
A movie van.

What kind of puzzle never sits still?
A jigglesaw puzzle.

FLICK PICKS

What is a duck's favorite movie?
"Quack to the Future."

What is a surgeon's favorite movie?
"Back to the Suture."

What is a dentist's favorite movie?
"Plaque to the Future."

What is a gymnast's favorite movie?
"Backbend to the Future."

What is a composer's favorite movie?
"Bach to the Future."

What Disney movie stars a dog who likes to jump up and down?

"Lady and the Tramp-oline."

What's a dimwit's favorite video game system?

Ninten-dodo.

WHERE'S R US

Where do you go to buy loud games?

Noise R Us.

Where do you go to buy a baby brother?

Boys R Us.

What song do you sing while playing Nintendo?

"Mario We Roll Along."

How did the composer sneak into the opera house?

Through the Bach door.

What do the children of classical musicians love to listen to?

Bach 'n' roll.

What's a Jedi's favorite musical instrument?
The Luk-ulele.

What's a ghoul's favorite musical instrument?
The spook-ulele.

What duet do police officers play on the piano?
Cop-sticks.

What duet do butchers play on the piano?
Chop-steaks.

What duet do Avon ladies play on the piano?
Lip-sticks.

What town has the most ballerinas?
Timbuktutu.

What would you get if you crossed a ballerina with a lighthouse?
A dancer who lights up every time she turns around.

What chubby men run the biggest circus in the world?
Barnum and Belly.

Who runs the biggest underwater circus in the world?
Barnacle and Bailey.

In what bedtime story do the bad guys live happily ever after?
An unfair-y tale.

How do you end a funny story?
"...and they lived happily ever laughter."

How do you end a story about frogs?
"...and they lived hoppily every after."

5.

Healthy, Wealthy, and Weird

What gangster rabbits held up banks?
Bunny and Clyde.

What gangster couple bungled every bank robbery they planned?
Bonnie and Clod.

YOU NAME IT

Where do you find the names of famous Hawaiian dancers?

In "Hula's Who."

Where do you find the names of famous ballerinas?

In "Tutu's Who."

Where do you find the names of famous lawyers?

In "Sue's Who."

Where do you find the names of famous twins?

In "Two's Who."

Where do you find the names of famous cooks?

In "Stew's Who."

Where do you find the names of famous people who fall asleep easily?

In "Snooze Who."

YOU NAME IT

Where do you find the names of famous ghosts?

In "Boo's Who."

Where do you find the names of famous crybabies?

In "Boo-hoo's Who."

Where do you find the names of famous Smurfs?

In "Blue's Who."

Where do you find the names of famous reporters?

In "News' Who."

Where do you find the names of famous witch doctors?

In "Voodoo's Who."

Where do you find the names of famous babies?

In "Goo-goo's Who."

What's the difference between your feet and your nose?

If your feet run, you're quick; but if your nose runs, you're sick.

Who was the most unfriendly pilgrim?
Miles Standoffish.

Why did the Lone Ranger hire a maid?
To polish the High Ho Silver.

Who snitches on people during Christmas?
Ebenezer Stooge.

How did Stephen King learn to write horror novels?
Trial and terror.

What did Telly Savalas write with?
A bald point pen.

What does a matador write with?
A bull point pen.

What is the most arrogant bird?
A cocky-too.

What is the craziest bird?
A kook-atoo.

Who was the toughest news-caster?
Walter Concrete.

Who was the most under-handed cowboy?
Billy the Cad.

What did the race horse champion wear under his clothes?
Jockey shorts.

What does Sylvester Stallone wear under his clothes?
Rocky shorts.

What short artist was Captain Kirk's biggest fan?
Toulouse Le Trekee.

How do you greet a rich baby?
"Gucci, Gucci, coo."

What do famous wolves become members of?
The Howl of Fame.

Where did prehistoric creatures shop?
At Dino Saurs and Roebuck.

What do you call the alligator in an Izod shirt?
A preptile.

6. Mad Mottoes & Screwy Slogans

What's a gardener's motto?
  A peony saved is a peony earned.

What's a barber's motto?
  Hairy today, gone tomorrow.

What's a boxer's motto?
  If at fist you don't succeed, try, try again.

What's a con artist's motto?
Cheat, drink, and be merry.

What's a justice of the peace's motto?
Eat, drink, and be married.

What's a sculptor's motto?
All work and no clay makes Jack a dull boy.

What's Rapunzel's motto?
Easy comb, easy grow.

What's Kleenex's motto?
Sneezy come, sneezy go.

What's the North Wind's motto?
Breezy come, breezy go.

What's Bonnie and Clyde's motto?
Crime is money.

What's Dr. Pepper's motto?
Thirst come, thirst served.

What's the Tinman's motto?
Oil's well that ends well.

What's Pinocchio's motto?
No nose is good nose.

What's every baby's motto?
If at first you don't succeed, cry, cry again.

What's a hockey player's motto?
The puck stops here.

What's a sheep's motto?
All's wool that ends wool.

What's a sheepherder's motto?
Shear and shear alike.

What's a ghost's motto?
Scare and scare alike.

What's a cyclop's motto?
Stare and stare alike.

What's a skunk's motto?
Eat, stink, and be merry.

What's a werewolf's motto?
Eat, drink, and be hairy.

What's a witch's motto?
Demons are a ghoul's best friend.

What's a horse's motto?
You get what you neigh for.

What's the marathon winner's motto?
He who hesitates is last.

What's the Roadrunner's motto?
Look before you beep.

What's a 747's motto?
If at first you don't succeed, fly, fly again.

What's a mink's motto?
If at fur you don't succeed, try, try again.

What's a soap company's motto?
Grime does not pay.

What's a cautious caterpillar's motto?
Look before you creep.

7. Childish and Wildish

Were do you learn how to take care of sick people?
In nurse-ery school.

Where do you learn how to become a hangman?
In noose-ery school.

What nursery rhyme character always messes
things up?
Mother Goof.

What nursery rhyme character has the cutest smile?
Dimple Simon.

What nursery rhyme character is always breaking out?
Pimple Simon.

Who is Casper the Friendly Ghost's favorite nursery rhyme character?
Little Boy Boo.

Who is Mr. Coffee's favorite nursery rhyme character?
Little Boy Brew.

What's a magician's favorite nursery rhyme?
Trickery, dickory, dock.

What's a virus' favorite childhood song?
"Pop Goes the Measle."

What's a semi-truck's favorite childhood song?
"Pop Goes the Diesel."

What professor emerged from a dark body of water covered with slime?
The Teacher from the Black Lagoon.

What did the jock say when he didn't understand a word the nerd said?
"It's all geek to me."

I'M GAME

What's a fisherman's favorite game?
  Row 'n' Tell.

What's a gardener's favorite game?
  Mow 'n' Tell.

What's a farmer's favorite game?
  Hoe 'n' Tell.

What's a tailor's favorite game?
  Sew 'n' Tell.

What's a salesperson's favorite game?
  Show 'n' Sell.

What's a lightning bug's favorite game?
  Glow 'n' Tell.

What do headhunters learn at day camp?
  Darts and crafts.

I'M GAME

What's a cheerleader's favorite game?
Show 'n' Yell.

What's a pitcher's favorite game?
Throw 'n' Tell.

What's a skunk's favorite game?
Show 'n' Smell.

What's a rooster's favorite game?
Crow 'n' Tell.

What's Jack Frost's favorite game?
Snow 'n' Tell.

What's Old Man River's favorite game?
Flow 'n' Tell.

What's the North Wind's favorite game?
Blow 'n' Tell.

What do Santa's reindeer learn in school?
Their Sleigh, B, Cs.

What does a little snake have when it doesn't get its way?

Hiss-terics.

What do choir students do after they finish their homework?

Their hymnwork.

What brand of crayon sobs at the drop of a hat?

Cry-ola.

UP THE HILL

What athletes went up the hill to fetch a pail of water?
Jock and Jill.

Who went up the hill on horseback to fetch a pail of water?
Jockey and Jill.

What bullies went up the hill to fetch a pail of water?
Jerk and Jill.

8. Fool-Time Jobs

How do you begin a detective story?
  "Once upon a crime…"

Where can you read about famous detectives?
  In "Clue's Who."

What did the lawyer say when he lost the court case?
  "If at first you don't succeed, trial, trial again."

When do barbers set their clocks ahead?
During daylight-shaving time.

When are tailors most difficult to be around?
When they're having a fit.

What does a chimney sweep wear to work?
Soot and tie.

What do women gardeners wear when they get married?
Weeding dresses.

What do women lifeguards wear when they get married?
Wading dresses.

What's a beautician's favorite pop group?
The Bleach Boys.

How did the Wright brothers know they'd be able to fly a plane?
Because where there's a Wilbur, there's a way.

What do undertakers carry their papers in?
Griefcases.

What's the difference between a presidential candidate and an overworked secretary?
One can't wait to get into office and one can't wait to get out of the office.

What would you get if you crossed an accountant,
a pickle, and Miss Universe?

A tall, green woman who can file taxes and her nails
at the same time.

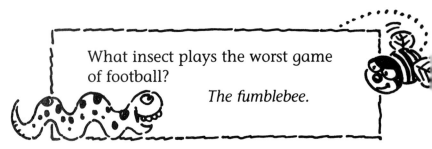

What insect plays the worst game
of football?

The fumblebee.

What are the worst baseball players members of?
The Hall of Shame.

Who solves mysteries while making coffee?
Nancy Brew.

What's a matador's favorite sport?
Basketbull.

What's a garbage collector's favorite sport?
Trash-basketball.

What famous painter never forgot anything?
Remembrandt.

Why did the artist yell?
He lost his tempera.

Why did the Japanese chef yell?
He lost his tempura.

What did the French chef give his girlfriend when he escorted her home?
A quiche goodnight.

In what wars did English teachers fight?
The Word Wars.

What would you get if you crossed an illustrator with an executioner?

An artist who draws pictures and then hangs them at dawn.

What would you get if you crossed a parachute with a distant relative?

A skydiver who drops in on you at the most inconvenient time.

What would you get if you crossed an acrobat with a Good Samaritan?

Someone who really bends over backward to help.

What do financial advisors sing when they sail off to sea?

"Bankers Away."

What banker snitches on his friends?

A tattle-teller.

Why did the actor need a calculator?

For audition and subtraction.

What actor can box and make smart financial decisions at the same time?

Investor Stallone.

What does a magician say when he takes a picture?

"Focus-pocus."

Who was the fastest magician that ever lived?

Hurry Houdini.

What would you get if you crossed a magician with a shopaholic?

Someone who makes money disappear.

What would you get if you crossed a police officer with a gambler?

A meter maid who gives out lottery tickets.

What would you get if you crossed a kitty, a hyena, and a millionaire?

A fat cat who laughs all the way to the bank.

What would you get if you crossed a rabbit with an amoeba?

A bunny that can multiply and divide itself.

What do boxers wear to tell time?

Fist watches.

How come Fred Flintstone could never become a firefighter?

He couldn't even put the cat out.

What are garbage collectors afraid of when the lights go out?

Things that go dump in the night.

TV or Not TV

What sourpuss watches TV all the time?
  A grouch potato.

Who sits in front of the TV with bad posture?
  A slouch potato.

What little kangaroo watches TV all day long?
A pouch potato.

What TV reruns star six spoiled kids who became brothers and sisters?
"The Bratty Bunch."

What daytime dramas do dummies watch?
Dope operas.

What's a duck's favorite TV rerun?
"I Love Goosey."

What cuddly bear hosts a talk show?
Winfrey-the-Pooh.

Where do candy-coated chocolates perform music videos?
On M & MTV.

What does Bullwinkle sing every December 25th?
  Christmoose carols.

Who fills cavities and gets into trouble?
  Dentist the Menace.

What's a boxer's favorite cable TV station?
  Knuckleodeon.

SOAP SCOOPS

What's Sir Lancelot's favorite soap opera?

"Guiding Knight."

What's Muhammad Ali's favorite soap opera?

"Guiding Fight."

What's a vampire's favorite soap opera?

"Guiding Bite."

What was Amelia Earhart's favorite soap opera?

"Guiding Flight."

GAME AND FORTUNE

What's a gymnast's favorite game show?

"Cartwheel of Fortune."

What's the Grinch's favorite game show?

"Wheel of Misfortune."

What's a baker's favorite cable TV station?
Pumper-Nickelodeon.

What's Fred and Wilma Flintstone's favorite rock band?
The Rolling Stone Age.

Where does Fred Flintstone get his hair cut?
At the Hanna Barber.

Does Fred Flintstone draw?
Sort of—he yabba-dabba doo-dles.

10. Oddities and Entities

What large, horned animal casts spells?
  A rhinosorceress.

Why was the mythical monster such a nuisance?
  He liked being the Centaur of attention.

What must you take if you want to ride Pegasus, the winged horse?
  Horseback gliding lessons.

Who is the Greek and Roman god of stupidity?
Jerkules.

What beauty contest did Venus, the goddess of love, win?
Myth Universe.

What is Zeus' favorite subject?
Mythematics.

What's the first thing Zeus puts on in the morning?
His thunderwear.

Who did ancient nerds worship?
Geek gods and goddesses.

Where did King Midas live after he retired?
In a gold age home.

What secret agent bleaches his hair?
James Blond.

Where did James Bond live after he retired?
In an old agent home.

What does James Bond do before he falls asleep?
  Goes undercovers.

What superheroine always messes things up?
  Blunder Woman.

What did the geek say to the mirror?
  "...Who's the squarest one of all?"

How do you wake up a dragon?
  With a fire alarm.

What knight wore tap shoes?
  Sir Dancelot.

What's a troll's favorite cowboy song?
  "Gnome on the Range."

Who serves ice cream faster than a speeding bullet?
  Scooperman.

Who makes mistakes faster than a speeding bullet?
  Blooperman.

Who is the strangest person in Emerald City?
  The Wizard of Odd.

How do you begin a story about a dummy?
"Dunce upon a time…"

Who got yelled at for breaking into a house owned by three bears?
Scoldilocks.

What fairy tale is about a snob and an ugly animal?
"Snooty and the Beast."

What princess cleaned for 100 years until she was kissed by a prince?
Sweeping Beauty.

What did Tinkerbell say to the mirror?
"…Who's the fairiest one of all?"

Why didn't Peter Pan always like Tinkerbell?
Because she was a fairy-weather friend.

What would you get if you crossed a rodent with Peter Pan?
A groundhog who looks for his shadow on February 2, but never finds it.

What did the Frankenstein monster read to the baby monster to help her fall asleep?
A feary tale.

What does the Frankenstein monster fly in?
Scareplanes.

Why was the Bride of Frankenstein always dieting?
She wanted to keep her ghoulish figure.

What sorceress thumbs rides on brooms?
A witchhiker.

What did Casper win for being the friendliest ghost?
A boo-by prize.

How do you begin a ghost story?
"Once upon a tomb..."

What do mummies wear on Halloween?
Cos-tombs.

What do mummies dance to?
Wrap music.

What biblical tale tells about a strongman who lost his strength when his hair was cut by a dishonest person?
Samson and Deliar.

What does King Kong do to succeed?
Puts his beast foot forward.

What's the difference between a needle and a cyclops?
They both have eyes, but a needle's easier to thread.

What's the difference between a cyclops and a needle?
They both have eyes, but a cyclops is easier to find in a haystack.

What do you get when you cross Toto with Godzilla?
A little monster that goes to Oz and swallows the Yellow Brick Road.

What shook under Dorothy and Toto's feet?
The Jello Brick Road.

What would you get if you crossed a vampire with an Avon lady?
I don't know, but when it rings the doorbell, don't answer it.

What would you get if you crossed Dracula with a termite?
A vampire who gets a wooden stake through his heart and then eats it.

Why did Dracula quit his job?
There was nothing there that he could sink his teeth into.

What web-footed friend played a vampire in the movies?
Bela Lagoosey.

What's the most frightening kind of bee?
A zom-bee.

Where do zombies live?
On dead-end streets.

What's a zombie's favorite sport?
Casketball.

What's a zombie's favorite party game?
Died 'n' Seek.

What's a ghost's favorite holiday song?
"I'm Dreaming of a Fright Christmas."

CLAUS TO HOME

What's Santa's favorite snack cake?
Ho-ho hos.

What does Santa put on his salad?
Elf-alfa sprouts.

Where does Santa park his reindeer?
Up on the hooftop.

What's a ghoul's favorite holiday song?
"I'll Be Gnome for Christmas."

What ghost is always welcome in December?
The Christmas Spirit.

What boxing title did King Kong try to win?
Heavyweight chimp.

Why were the animals on the ark angry at its builder?
Because he acted like a Noah-it-all.

How did Noah get ballerinas onto the ark?
Tutu-by-tutu.

How did Noah get wrecked cars onto the ark?
Tow-by-tow.

What phone company do aliens use to call home?
E.T.&T.

What do Martians roast at campfires?
Marsmallows.

What do witches spread on their bagels?
Scream cheese.

What do witches read to their babies to help them sleep?
Scary tales and dreadtime stories.

Party Animals

What Australian animal loves to dance?
The tangoroo.

What do dancers climb?
Fred Astairs.

What do Fred and Wilma Flintstone dance to?
Bedrock 'n' roll music.

What do astronauts dance to?
Rocket 'n' roll music.

What music do Smurfs dance to?
The blues.

What's a tornado's favorite dance?
The twist.

What's a garbage collector's favorite dance?
The trashcan-can.

What's a pessimist's favorite dance?
The can't-can't.

What do truck drivers do when the music starts?
Brakedancing.

How do hens and roosters dance?
Chick-to-chick.

Who did the monster take to the dance?
His girlfiend.

What does Mr. Spock perform at parties?
Magic treks.

Did the stick of dynamite enjoy the party?
Yes, it had a blast.

PUN AND GAMES

What's a fussbudget's favorite game?
Par-choosy.

What's a vampire's favorite game?
Follow the bleeder.

What's a librarian's favorite game?
Follow the reader.

What's a lazy toad's favorite game?
Sleep frog.

What's a baby mountain climber's favorite game?
Peak-a-boo.

What's a baby thief's favorite game?
Sneak-a-boo.

What does a thief wear to a fancy party?
A mink stole-n.

How do you keep a gorilla from crashing your party?
Send him an invitation.

What Native American loved to dance?
Polka-hontas.

Who was the wittiest Native American?
Joke-ahontas.

Why did Casper get all dressed up for the party?
He was the ghost of honor.

What did Cinderella's pet seal wear to the ball?
A glass flipper.

Who helped the cow go to the ball?
Its dairy godmother.

HIDE AND SEEK

What's a bee's favorite game?
Hive 'n' Seek.

What's a justice of the peace's favorite game?
Bride 'n' Seek.

What's a doctor's favorite game?
Hide 'n' Sick.

What's a nerd's favorite game?
Hide 'n' Geek.

What's an undertaker's favorite game?
Formaldehyde 'n' Seek.

What's a peeping Tom's favorite game?
Hide 'n' Peek.

What's a con artist's favorite game?
Lied 'n' Sneak.

What pirate sets the table at formal dinner parties?
Long John Silverware.

Why did the bride ask the Smurf to bring a library book to her wedding?

So she'd have something borrowed and something blue.

What's the difference between a Jack-in-the-Box and a party crasher?

One pops out when the music stops, and one pops in when the music starts.

What musical instrument did Daniel Boone play?

The tromboone.

What alligator plays the electric guitar at parties?

The rockodile.

What is a Smurf's favorite holiday?

Blue Year's Eve.

Did you ever ask yourself this silly question:

How does a dragon blow out his birthday candles?

Why do flies carry stopwatches at parties?

Because flies time when they're having fun.

12. Last Laughs

What car can't stop talking?
Chatty Chatty Bang Bang.

What does Chitty Chitty Bang Bang blow its nose in?
A Honk-erchief.

What are cars afraid of when the lights go out?
Things that go bumper in the night.

How did James Bond get to work every morning?
He took the spyway.

What did the angry king shout to the disloyal car?
"Off with her head-light!"

What green cars live in sewers?
Teenage Mutant Ninja Tercels.

What are championship pickup trucks members of?
The Haul of Fame.

What is a semi's favorite sport?
Truck and field.

What sound does a Tonka truck's horn make?
"Honka!"

What car lives in a bell tower?
The Hatchback of Notre Dame.

When does poison ivy get caught in traffic?
During rash hour.

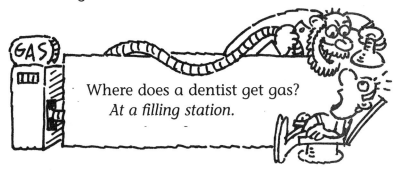

Where does a dentist get gas?
At a filling station.

Why did the Easter Bunny get a ticket?
For running a hop sign.

What is the difference between a parade float and a kitchen sink?
You can sink a float, but you can't float a sink.

What's the difference between a red carpet and a deodorant stick?
One you roll out and the other you roll on.

What would you get if you crossed Einstein with a sleepwalker?
A lazy student who gets A's while getting ZZZ's.

What did the ship say when asked when it wanted to sail?

"The schooner the better."

At what motel does Charlie the Tuna stay?

The Holiday Finn.

How does Moby Dick like his steak cooked?

Whale done.

In what part of California do wealthy fish live?

Beverly Gills.

Which ocean won the race?

Neither, they tide.

What's a tornado's favorite song?

"Blow, blow, blow your boat...."

What natural disaster moves too fast to be seen clearly?

A blurricane.

What colorful clown appears in the sky after a storm?

Rainbozo.

What do you get when you subtract one Parthenon from another Parthenon?

Parthe-none.

What did one volcano say to the other volcano?
"I lava you."

What would you get if you crossed a Boy Scout with his grandmother?
Someone who can help himself across the street.

What would you get if you crossed Babe Ruth with a fugitive?
A baseball player who hits the ball and then runs away from home.

What would you get if you crossed an ostrich with a mobster?
A long-necked gangster who buries someone else's head in the sand.

What Canadian police officer resembles four U.S. presidents?

Mountie Rushmore.

What did the tree deposit in the bank?

Its leaf savings.

What tree owns a chocolate factory?

Willow Wonka.

What mistakes can't be explained?

The Seven Blunders of the World.

FLOWER POWER

What flowers do you send a squirrel on Valentine's Day?
Forget-me-nuts.

What flowers do you send a snake?
Hissanthemums.

What flowers do you send a ballerina?
Tutulips.

What flowers do you send a fish?
Pe-tunas.

What flowers do you send a comedian?
Laughodils.

What flowers do you send a Russian king?
Czarnations.

What flowers do you send Pinocchio?
Lie-lacs.

What does your true love give to you on the last day of Fall?

A partridge in a bare tree.

Where do you bring a snowman that's not yours?

To the Frost and Found.

When do birds like to play outside?

On worm days.

Why did the chicken walk to the grocery store?

Because it didn't have change for a bus.

When does a poisonous snake bite?
When it's hissed off.

Why wouldn't Pinocchio go camping?

He was afraid a Boy Scout would rub his legs together.

What law did Sir Isaac Newton discover while in his dentist's office?

The law of cavity.

What did the robber say to the queen bee?

"Your honey or your life."

Who lives in the coldest part of the backwoods?
Chillbillies.

Why did Pocahontas excuse herself?
She had to go to the pow-wowder room.

What Native American tribes celebrate Christmas?
The Navaho-ho-hos.

What Native American brought down the Ten Commandments?
Geronimoses.

What does Geronimo do when he's sad?
Geronimopes.

Why was the mother star disappointed when she had a little daughter?
She wanted a little sun.

Why did the baby moon get punished?
For staying out all night.

What did the meteorite say when asked to give a quote?
"No comet."

Index